MW00626055

Printed in the United States of America.
First Printing, 2021

Publisher
Williams Commerce, LLC
Visit Our Website
Williamscommerce1.com
ISBN: 978-1-7376488-0-2

Contents

Intro

First, I would like to say Thank You for taking this journey with me. These pieces were all specifically hand-selected for this book. Every word in this book has helped me heal through the traumas of my past. There are a few pieces that are not even poems at all; they are letters. Each of these pieces are weights that have been lifted from My Soul. These are My Truths that are no longer secrets hiding within me. These are also the Collective Truths of those I have loved and had to watch suffer and try to survive as I was and ALWAYS Will Do...Survive Today to Thrive Tomorrow!

These poems can also be seen as entries. You can take this journey however you want. If you want to read it the way it is written, go ahead. If you're willing to take a risk and read them by date, go ahead. Regardless of which path you take to finish, the destination is the same. For example, this journey can be read in order because it's from My Soul's order despite the dates, or you can try to take the journey of reading this by chronological date. The journey is within finding them. Enjoy! YOU ARE THE MASTER OF YOUR FATE! Be Great. Have Gratitude. Be Greatfull!

I hope these pieces bring you as much peace to know that you are NEVER alone in life, no matter whatever it is. There is ALWAYS someone there who understands you no matter how far they may seem. I hope these words bring you as much freedom as they brought me when writing them in My Journey of Becoming the Amazing Black Woman I am Today and Destined to Be. You are not alone in your struggle, no matter how alone you may feel. I hope these words serve as a reminder. I hope these words can help change your life for the better in whatever shape they need to.

I Love You!

TRIGGER WARNING
Some pieces talk about Self-Harm, Sexual Assault, and Rape.

Please keep an eye out for ** next to the titles because this is your Trigger Warning.
TRIGGER WARNING

Lastly, Thank You Again for taking this journey into a part of my life.

Always
I Love You,
Whylde Chylde

Who Is The Real Me?

What do you see when you look at me

Do you see me

Or the me I want you to see

We are all one person

But who is the real me

The me I see

Is broken

She worthless

When I look into her dark brown eyes

I see the pain

She holds in her soul

The me I see

Has been beaten down

By the world

And destroyed by those closest to her

Yet,

That is not what I want you to see

I want you to see

The love she has

And the happiness
In her beautiful deep brown eyes
The value she holds
And the peace she brings

I want you to see me
Not the me I see
But the me I want to be
The me I used to be
Before I changed
Because of the cruel hand that life had dealt

Who am I really
Is the real me
A beautiful broken girl
With pain in her soul
And love in heart
Is this the real me

Who am I really
Am I really the me I see
Or am I the me I want to be
Who am I really

All of them or none of them

Who am I really

I am the Me that I choose to be

Love,

Whylde Chylde

June 2018

The Untold Story

BY: _Whylde Chylde_
June 12, 2018

The first time you touched me, I was 11 years old. And that's all it was, a touch, you molested me. When you touched me, I told you to stop, and you did. I don't remember where you touched me though. You left me alone, but you left me feeling bad for telling you to stop, yet I knew that I didn't like what you did. That was not my only first that day. That was the first time I cut myself. At 11, I didn't know what I was doing, yet somehow, I was so methodical about it when I did it.

I remember how I got a broken piece of glass that came from a small perfume bottle. I took my time to examine my body, and for some reason, I chose my arm. My right arm, a little bit low on the inside of it, to be exact. It was a small cut, but it was all that I needed back then. It felt sensational, but it hurt at the same time. The pain was nothing compared to the pleasure that I felt. In fact, it was euphoric.

You didn't start touching me again until I was 12. This time around, you waited until I was asleep. I know because I woke up to you in my bed. The other you inside of my underwear, you were rubbing yourself against me. I remember waking up feeling...Scared. Frightened because I didn't know what to do. Confused because I didn't know why you were in my bed rubbing yourself on me. However, not quite surprised that it was YOU who was in my bed. So, I froze and did the only thing I could think of and pretend to be asleep. I tried to shift my body to make it harder for you. But you finished anyways, inside my underwear. And that was the beginning of what many of my nights would become. I don't know how many nights I endured this.

Sometime after that, I started cutting myself periodically. When I first started, it was to release the pain, take it from the inside and bring it out. For a while, it was working. The physical pain brought me pleasure. This pleasure, in a sense, allowed me to feel something other than grey, but none of you could tell because I was still smiling every day and pretending everything was okay, when in fact, it wasn't. I felt like I was slowly dying on the inside, but I didn't know it at the time. All I really knew was that cutting took some of the pain away.

And for some reason, I vaguely remember you touching me in different parts of the house when I lived in Washington State when we were alone. But I remember the nights because I used to fall asleep in the fetal position hoping that tonight would be the night, I didn't wake up with you in my bed. Some nights I was lucky, but not every night.

When I was 13, on Cultural Night, you took things a step further. That night, you went all the way. I don't remember much about that night, but I remember you somehow convinced me to take my clothes off and lay on my carpet. I laid with my head by my door, it was on my left, and my closet was by the other side. My mattress was not too far from my lower half. I remember laying on my bedroom floor with my shirt and legs open and you between them. I remember feeling the tip you tried to push through my lips. I remember you trying to push your way through my barrier. I said ouch and asked you to stop, and I crawled back a little. You followed me by crawling forward and trying to push yourself past my barrier once more. And again, I crawled back, and you followed. I remember feeling the wall space between my door and closet hovering above my head. You tried to push yourself past my barrier once more, and I remember mentally leaving my body and watching myself. I remember staring at my own face, curious about what I was looking at that held my attention so much. Throughout the whole ordeal, I was just watching my face from above, just wondering what could possibly be so interesting that I was just so lost in it. I don't know if you finished in me or literally on me, because I remember wiping myself down and changing my underwear because it was wet, and I knew I couldn't wear it again. I was on autopilot for the rest of the night. And when I had to, I acted like everything was okay and that I was alright. Despite being confused at what happened to me earlier that night before she came to pick us up for my performance.

I'm pretty sure that this was the night you got me pregnant too. I didn't realize it until I woke up in the middle of a random night because I had to throw up. I never realized that my period was late. It wasn't something I paid attention to or ever felt that it was something I needed to keep track of. However, earlier that day, I thought it was weird that I kept smelling eggs and all my burps tasted like boiled eggs, especially since I hadn't eaten any in the forthcoming weeks, maybe even months. I didn't pay much attention to it until that very night when I was awakened from my sleep because I had the sudden urge to vomit. I was 13 years old, and I didn't know what to do. So, the next time you found your way to my bed like I knew you would, and trust me, I didn't have to wait long either, I told you that I was pregnant. I remember the words left my mouth before I had a chance to do anything; a chance to think it over, whether I really wanted to tell you, a chance to think about it, and what I could do. I regretted saying something the moment it left my mouth.

At 13, I somehow had the money to pay for a pregnancy test. I gave you the money because, at that tender age, I didn't know how to buy one. You bought a box with two tests inside. We took them both. The first was positive, and the second was negative. When we were done, we put them in a plastic bag and threw them away in the backyard. You gave her the news. Then she yelled at me and interrogated me pressing to find out who I 'slept' with. But that was a trick question for two reasons; the first, because I didn't sleep with anyone, they slept with me. And second, I didn't know how to tell her that it was you. I was scared because I didn't know what you told her, and I didn't know how she would take it or if she would have even believed me. But I never said a word.

She gave me a test. She asked me what I was going to do. At 13, these were my options: get rid of it or have your baby. I told her that I would get rid of it because that was easier than having your baby, and that was the last time we had a conversation about it. However, that was not the last time she had asked me about who. And that was the beginning of me being presumed a whore. Why you ask, because I was pregnant and I didn't know who the father was, or so she thought. My favorite answer was I don't know whenever I wanted to avoid something. I "I don't know'd" her until she got tired of asking and never getting a straight answer, or any answer for that matter. I remember how she threatened to come up to my school and tell them that I was pregnant to find out who the culprit was. I used to think she was lying about me being pregnant to intimidate me into saying something, and a few times, I almost cracked and said something, but not on you. I was going to lie and make up a name because I didn't want to drag anyone into my problem.

Still, to this very day, I don't know what happened. I don't know if I was pregnant, not for a fact, at least. But I have always had that voice in the back of my head telling me that I was. If I was, I don't know if I had a miscarriage or if she found a way to give me an at-home abortion. During that time, I tried to ignore and block out as much as I could. Yet, for some reason, I like to take comfort in the thought that I had a miscarriage. Maybe it's because I hate that feeling in my gut when I think about how I know that I was pregnant.

My cutting started getting worse. I didn't always cut myself soon afterward. Sometime after THAT night, it became more frequent, not the full thing, just business as usual. However, you did do some new things, like instead of it being in my room sometimes we were in yours. Once, you convinced me to try this thing. You told me to grab the lotion, and I did. You put the lotion on yourself. I don't remember when I pulled my pants down, but I know you asked me. I remember being on my knees and feeling you quickly pushing your way into my anal cavity. I remember the grueling pain; I remember how fast it was. I remember that it was even more than when you decided to have sex with my body, even though it didn't last long.

Then I stopped cutting myself, and it was not because I wanted to do so. I needed that physical pain. Back then, I never realized how much I needed it. I stopped because one day she and him caught me, or I might have asked for help. To be honest, it could have been a little bit of both. Either way, I had cut too deep accidentally, and I got scared because I was bleeding more than ever, and it wouldn't stop. It barely slowed down, and I saw my tissue turn red from my blood. It was a big diagonal cut on my left forearm. I will never forget what she said when she came into my room.

She told me, "You're doing this for attention..." After that, I stopped listening because hearing that broke something in me that day, and I still don't know what it is. Maybe because I felt like she took the only real thing that made me feel safe away. She took it and made it dirty like you made me. I didn't cut myself again after that day (*until ten years later). Even though I thought about it and still do on my most extremely rough days. On the roughest days, I was ready to give up. And I tried, more than once, and I wasn't even going to leave a note.

The following summer, I told a friend a little bit of what you did to me. And they told someone else, and you know how the game of 'Telephone' is played.

Eventually, they all found out and someone told me that the cops were going to be involved, and that was the last thing I wanted. Therefore, I did the only thing I felt I could do, which was tell everyone that I lied and made it all up.

Initially, I only told someone to get it off my chest. The situation was wearing me down and consuming me. I only wanted you to stop, not go to jail. When we returned to school, I didn't hear any rumors, but I knew they were floating around.

When I came back from New York that summer, you never spoke to me. You didn't look at me, I didn't exist in your world anymore, but you still existed in mine. You treated me like I was invisible, and sometimes that's what hurt the most, more than the abuse itself. Even though it did help me to push and lock the memories away. It has been over five years, and you still have not spoken to me.

We didn't speak until Summer 2019, 11 years, and he messaged me on Snapchat

Now, most of my scars have faded, but some remain. I counted 11 (06/01/18). *NOW (03/22/2020) I have three more, one on my hand and two more on my arm.

The Night I Met Shadow

By: _Whylde Chylde_

June 17, 2018

I never understood why your nickname was Shadow. I liked it, even though I never called you 'Shadow' often. However, when I did, it felt like it was a sweet innocent secret between you and me, and I liked that too. I never realized then that you would become a shadow, my 'Shadow' at that.

It's weird when I think about it now because I felt like you were my 'Shadow,' but when I thought of it, of you, in that aspect, it was sweet. It, you, made me smile.

Every time I ask you about that night, you seem slightly annoyed that I'm asking you about it again. However, every time you tell me it's like it's the first time, I'm hearing it. So how can you TRULY blame me for it? Especially when we don't even really remember it in the same way. The way you remember is not the same way I remember it. This is how I remember...

Tuesday- August 22, 2017

...I went Downtown with a couple of friends. We had a girl's date. We had dinner, drinks, and went to the movies. We had a drink, and two shots, one of which was free. We finished up and had a couple of hours to kill before the movie. We went to Sephora and spent some time there. Then we went to the bar across the street, it was O'Keefe Bar and Grill, and we all got one more drink. I had a Long Island Iced Tea, and it was good, but I'm a slow drinker, plus I had paid $12 for it. I didn't want to waste my money on a drink I liked. So, we had 15 more minutes until the movie started, and I still had a good portion of my drink left. I spent those next 15 minutes focusing on finishing the drink, and we left for the movies. I don't even remember what movie we saw. I remember while walking to the bathroom, I hurt my hip badly. I don't remember how or on what, but all I do know is that I walked into something because I felt the constant pain there reminding me. I vaguely remember texting you after or during the movie and somewhat on the ride over.

I vaguely remember being on the 103 buses on my way to your house. *I now remember that I fell asleep for most of the ride (03/22/2020)*

[*You came and got me off the bus. My hands were all over you. I waited for you upstairs. You sent your friends home and came upstairs. We talked. I told you to grab a condom. While your back was turned, I got butt-ass naked because I took my dress off. More than likely, I did not have panties on. I laid on my back with my legs wide open in the air. Waiting for you. You put the condom on and got on top of me.*]

I vaguely remember you on top of me, stroking me. In my mind, when I remember that night, you're a shadow. A shadow of yourself. A shadow of a man, I thought I knew and trusted.

[*You were giving me the best dick of my life. It was so good; I was planning out our future together. You asked to switch positions*, but I was too drunk to be in another position except on my back. **We had sex in that position for about 45 minutes. I would not let you get off me****]

I now remember telling you "No" to switching positions because I knew I was too drunk to be in any other position or else I would have thrown up (03/22/2020)

You had sex with me, you assaulted me, you raped me

I do not understand how I am 5 '3" and have never weighed more than 135lbs in my entire life but could stop you from letting you off me. You are a WHOLE foot taller than me, and damn sure weighs more than I do even when you're at your lightest.

I vaguely remember you giving me one of your black shirts. I vaguely remember you handing me a cup, *and 03/22/2020 now I remember it was water*. I vaguely remember you waking me up to smoke. I remember trying to go back to sleep but couldn't because I felt nauseous. I vividly remember jumping out of your bed having to run to the bathroom to throw up. I vaguely remember going back to sleep.

I remember you waking me up to smoke again. I remember taking a couple of hits. I remember waking up and running to the bathroom to throw up again. I vaguely remember you driving me home in the morning. I remember throwing up in my bathroom all morning. That is everything that I remember from that day on Tuesday, August 22, 2017.

What I remember is a 'Shadow.' Now, I know why you were always my 'Shadow.' I trusted you and still kind of do. I don't know why, but I do know that I shouldn't trust you anymore. You're not safe anymore, and to be honest, you never were, because looking back now *03/22/2020* I had met 'Shadow' already. I met 'Shadow' in bits and pieces whenever we had sex. But 'Shadow' did not formally introduce himself until that very night. * Because how can you truly trust a Shadow; you were never there to begin with.

[I was begging for you to have sex with me. I would not take no for an answer. I baited. Every time you tried to get off me, I would pull you back. I was in control. You gave me what I

wanted. What guy would say No, especially when "I" kept saying yes. It was all me.]

You have a whole foot and one-hundred pounds on me. You were sober. I don't understand how this happened. I trusted you, and you took advantage. Now I don't know what to do, and don't know how to feel.

I know what did not happen. We did not have regret sex because how can I regret something that I don't remember because that is not what this feels like. I know what you did was rape, but that is also not what this feels like. I feel like you took advantage of me, but in this case, isn't that what taking advantage is…rape.

How is that possible? What am I supposed to do with that? How do I even begin to be okay if it's my fault for putting us in that position? *But now (03/22/2020), I understand that no matter what I did, I did not deserve for you to take advantage of me, for you to rape me for 45 minutes, and it's crazy because you told me it was 45 minutes long because I don't remember, even until this day. You're still a shadow when I remember it, but now, I know it is really you.*

I should have known better, but so should you. My biggest regret was going to your house that night, and none of this would have happened. *But now (03/22/2020), My biggest regret is meeting you, _ _ _ _ _ _ 'Shadow' _ _ _ _ _ _ _ _ _ _ _ _ _!

[And I don't know if you are aware, but these sections are filled with your words that are filling in the missing pieces from my memory. These are only a few of the things that I remember that you have told me.]

In the Shadows

I can feel the monsters

Hiding

In the shadows

Waiting for the perfect moment

To strike

Waiting for when I'm at my lowest

To get me

I can feel the monsters

Hiding

In the shadows

Following my every move

Trying to grab me

Walking close behind me

But not so close that you can actually grab me

I can feel the monster

Hiding

In the shadows

Breathing on my neck

But when I look behind me

He's not there

I can feel the monster

Hiding

In the shadows

He's big and strong

Hard to miss

But when I turn around,

He's gone

I can still feel the monster

Hiding

In the shadows

Love,

Whylde Chylde

June 2018

A Friend

Would a friend hurt another
Like you did to me
When at their most vulnerable
And needed protection

Would a friend take advantage?
The same way
You took advantage of me
When you knew better

Would a friend blame another
For their actions
In order to make themselves feel better
At my expense

Would a friend laugh and joke
About something that hurts
A friend, hurts me
Like it was nothing serious

A real friend would never
We were never really friends

You used me
For you

Love,
Whylde Chylde
June 17, 2018

You Then Me

When you came into my life

You were not what I expected

The person I met

Is not the person I got

When we spoke

You made me feel

Like it was only me

And you

When we were laid up together

You filled me in more ways than one

You made me feel whole

When I knew that I wasn't

When you saw my brokenness

You cherished me

Because you were broken too

Together we felt whole

When you gave me some of your pieces

I took them all

And gave you my best parts
In exchange

It was a fair trade, so I thought
Because you had more broken pieces than me
I fixed you, at least I tried to
When you only broke me further

I loved you. At least I tried
While you hurt me
I cared for you. I thought no one else was
When you belittle me

When you saw I was ready to quit
The you I met came back
You held onto me
Convinced me

Despite all the voices
Telling me no
Despite all the feelings of needing to leave
Yet still, I stayed for you

It was never about me

It was always about you

Even when you made it look like it wasn't

It still really was

Love,

Whylde Chylde

June 17, 2018

The Story of Harlem

By: _Whylde Chylde_

September 28, 2018

I came over after work like usual. We smoked, talked, watched tv, all like normal. And like usual, you would touch me, which I didn't mind because it was never intrusive. You would stop after I would ask a few times, but that day was not like usual. It started out like normal, which is precisely why I didn't see it coming. Like usual, you found your way inside my underwear, but it was in such an unusual place. Like usual, you tested the water, and I said no. You kept trying, like usual, and I told you to stop. And you kept trying, and that's what was unusual.

(I should have realized at that moment that you were not going to stop. And I should have fought you off instead of just lying there.) And again, I told you to stop but with only a whisper because that's when it happened.

I remember I began to crawl away from you slowly. I remember crawling from the center of your bed to the right corner because that was the direction I was facing towards the door. The whole time I'm crawling away, you were still trying to continue to force your way in. And you were speaking to me because I remember hearing your voice, but I couldn't hear a single word you were saying. All I could hear was my own voice barely above a whisper, pleading for you to stop. I remember you found your way in. I finally remember reaching the corner of your bed with tears in my eyes, realizing that you were not going to stop. I remember my body became so weak it felt like I was dead. It was like all my strength had suddenly just left my body. I laid there looking at your door, hoping someone...anyone would knock or come in. I don't remember if you finished or not. And if you did, I don't know where either, to be honest. I don't even remember getting up or what we did next or the rest of the night. I don't know how long I stayed after.

And I don't even remember much of the next day. But I do remember NOT feeling like myself. I do remember you kept asking what was wrong the next day. And I remember answering "I don't know" and giving some bullshit excuse that came out my mouth. But I remember thinking to myself, 'What do you mean what's wrong? You hurt me yesterday, and I'm hurting even still 'till now' every single time you asked me, not even actually realizing what happened. The whole time you were expecting me to cheer up and be happy and enjoy the fact that you were catering to me. How could I when you hurt me in such a bad way and could not even say you're sorry?

Still to this very day, I couldn't say what you did to me out loud *I can say it, you raped me, but I still cannot say where it was (03/22/2020) *

*(10/11/2020) * I can finally say it now. You, _ _ _ _ _ _ _ 'Harlem' _ _ _ _ _ _ _ _ _ _ _ _ _sodomized me.

Do I Haunt You

Do I haunt you
The same way
You haunt me

Do you see
Bits of me
In everyone around

I can see
The pieces of you
In the faces

Can you see
The resemblance of
Me in them

Are the memories like
Getting drenched
With ice-cold water

Do they have you
Frozen in place

With steam rolling off you

Do you get nervous
Around people, scared
That you might see me

We were both there
But it was different
For each of us

I can just tell
It changed
The both of us

You took something from me
But it took way more from you
It was mine but I'm better off without it

So, Do I Haunt You
The same way
You haunt me

Love,

Whylde Chylde

September 2019

A Soul With An Angry Heart

My heart is angry

My soul is on fire

I am mad at the world

That life goes on

As time continues

I am stuck

In a dark place

All alone

No one can hear me

I am invisible

Begging for help

Arms extended

Grasping

At the emptiness

In the air

And the nothingness

In the dark skies

Hoping

Someone can save me

Knowing

I can only save myself

But

With lungs filled

I am drowning

It's not water

And I am gasping

For oxygen

Or something

Anything

That resembles air

To bring me back

Back to life

I am dead inside

Weighed down

From the pressure

Crushed

By the pain

Shattered to pieces

Barely held together

Yet

Forced to push through

With a smile on my face

Like nothing is wrong

I am slowly dying

On the inside

But I am fighting

To live

For another day

To see

The beauty

When it's no longer grey

To feel

The warmth

Of love

Not the fire

From the anger

That lies within

And resides in my soul

Love,

Whylde Chylde

June 2018

A Body and A Soul

How do you bring a soul back

From the land of the dead

To a body that is broken

Beyond repair

A soul filled with nothing

But the blackness

Of despair

A soul drowning

Surrounded by tears

Caused from pain

To a body

That is shattered

Like glass

A body

Barely held together

At the seams

A body too weak

From the battle of life
To hold that soul

A body and soul precisely
Designed for one another
But too damaged be with each other

Empty alone trying to fit back together
And even emptier apart
So how do you bring an empty soul back
To a broken body damaged beyond repair

Love,
Whylde Chylde
July 28, 2018

The Story of Death

Have you ever imagined Death

The way it sounds

Ever hear silence

Or lack thereof

The pure utter silence

Well except the sound of you

Or should I say me

Ever imagined the way it felt

Death, I mean

It feels like time stood still

Well except everything around you

Again, I mean, Me

Think of being frozen in a time and space

A place where you can't be reached

Imagine this

....

Nothing

....

Well except you

....

Me

....

Just nothingness

Now imagine the journey to Death

How you're ripped from yourself

Me from myself

Out of nowhere

I couldn't make a sound

And unable to move

Physically just stuck there

But now there's two of you

Two of me

The us who's stuck in nowhere

The one who's frozen

And the one that moves on

Because we have to go somewhere

With Death

Have you ever thought of

Where that place is

What it's like

Or maybe even where
The consciousness of you
I mean me goes, you know
To be with Death, of course

Death takes us
To another nowhere
Its where Death lives
The place of Nowhere
To be isolated
To talk to no one but you
Sorry, I mean Me

I have never imagined death
At least, not to be like that
Or have I since I wrote this
Maybe Death is more peaceful than that
One can hope, right
Death isn't violent
Or is it

Everyone has imagined Death
And what it would be like

But many don't know

While many do know

Yet, everyone's Death is different

And we are all alone

With Death, I mean

Love,

Whylde Chylde

February 25, 2019

Hindsight

Why was it so easy for you to hurt me
But so hard for me to pick up the pieces
The pieces of me that you left behind
You left me there like I meant nothing
As if I was nothing

I'm only left with the memories
And the memories hurt
Because I can see what I couldn't before
I have hindsight vision
And the picture is clearer now

I saw you but you never saw me
I wanted to save you from yourself
You wanted to sink your hooks in me
You reeled me in
Nice and slow

You built me up for you
And broke me down from me
You saw how fragile I was already
You knew it would be easy to break me into pieces

47

You had me

It was easy to you
Almost like a game
You played it so well
I didn't even know
There was a game to even be played

You set the trap
And I played right into your hands
Easy pickings
It happened so quick that I didn't see it
But I felt it

I didn't know what it was
Until I knew
I tried to pick up the pieces
But it's painful
The edges are sharp

You made them that way
Then walked away
You didn't look back

You left me to clean up your mess

Why was it so easy for you to hurt me

Love,

Whylde Chylde

June 2018

A Heart Full of Its Own Pieces

My heart is full

It aches with love and pain

Pain that I caused

It hurts

Cause it's shattered

Not because of you

The pieces came

Long before you

They've been chipped away

Thinking that

I still had

Those lost pieces

Trying to put a new heart together

With what I thought were

My shards and they were

They were mine

From when my heart was full

Whole

But they no longer belong to me
Cause they were the pieces
That now belonged to the sculptor

The ones who came before you
They had my heart
And they chipped away at me

Took the parts
And pieces
For their art

They left me
With my own scraps
A heart full of its own pieces

Covered with tape
Destined to break
Fragile as a newborn baby

On its way to its deathbed

And this was my heart
Held together with holes and brittle bones

So, when I gave you
My heart
Out of pure love

It was in a capsule
Tainted, barely held together
Stuck in a war

With itself
My love trying to fill in the pieces
For a heart still in pieces

I love you
But it comes from a broken heart
Not that kind of broken

But broken from the years
Of letting too many
Too many artists have their way

So, when I found you
The sculptor of my dreams
I gave you the rest of me

Even if it meant
Giving you my broken heart
A heart full of its own pieces

Love,
Whylde Chylde
May 10, 2020

Faces of Black Trauma

The faces of Black trauma

It's multifaceted.

From the little black boy

Who lost his smile

Because to the world,

He's a man.

And there's no more #BlackBoyJoy

To the little Black girl

Whose laugh can light up the world

With the twinkle that can be seen from outer space

Yet, she somehow, she always goes missing

So, there's no laughter in her soul

Only darkness hiding in the depths

It is the Black man

Trying to go home

After a long day at the office

Somehow being mistaken for another

Because he fit the description

And the description is nigger

By the same pig that's going to lock him up

And treat him like he's the animal.

It's the Black woman
Loving and protecting her King
When she should be protecting herself
From that same King
Because he's taking her love for granted
Leaving her with scars
And then calling her bitter

The Black father
Trying to be a father
All the while being called a deadbeat
By the same person who is too immature to co-parent
So, he's not allowed to see his kids
Unless it's on her terms
Because their child is her pawn

And the Black mother
Who is always worried
But can never show it.
She stays up late
Worried about her loved ones

Because she never knows

If this is going to be the last goodbye, she tells her
family

Before they leave the house and face the world

With the possibilities of them never returning home

Love,

Whylde Chylde

August 26, 2019

Motherly Love

You were supposed to teach me love.

What it looks like

And how it feels.

Yet, your love seems to hurt.

Your love can be toxic.

Because it punishes when you're not happy,

And lashes out when it's not going your way.

The love overflows when you want something.

If I am being honest,

You did teach me how to love,

But it was your version.

The version that hurts just as much as it doesn't.

You are the love that I seek,

And the hate that I find.

It is the warmth of your love that I can feel,

That is surrounded by the cold chill of negativity.

Your love can feel so good

And feel so bad at the same time.

I loved it,
And I hated it.

I managed to get the best parts of your love
And some of the worst parts.
I want to keep the parts of the love that's pure
And leave the tainted parts behind.

You're my role model.
My guidance.
The person that I love,
You are where I came from.

We are so similar.
Yet, so different.
You are my mother.
And I am your daughter.

You are what I need to leave behind,
Not because I don't love you;
It's because your love hurts,
And I need to love me more than I love you.

In order to be able to save myself.

Love,

Whylde Chylde

January 16, 2020

The Sky Is Falling

The sky was stolen

But it's still blue

Filled with clouds

And shedding tears

Because it's lost

Just looking for a way

To the familiarity of home

The sun is out

Its gleam is gone

No brightness in its eyes

It has lost its shine,

And the twinkle in its soul

Wandering and wondering

Where to go

Since it can't go back

To the place, it once has known

The sky was stolen

At a moment's notice

It feels like it's dying

Because it's no longer flying

Taking the birds with it
But the wind protects them
From meeting their end

There is no sky
But there is still wind
Pushing it to its new home
One breeze at a time
The freshness of each gust
And the crisp of new air
Destination unknown
The winds guidance to find its way
To the place where it needs to go

A new place to called home

Love,
Whylde Chylde
February 25, 2019

They Say

They say
If you've been on the receiving end
Of police brutality
Or assault, then
They say
You have to let it go.

They say
If you don't let it go
Then it's going to consume you.
They say
You have too
Or else the rage will hold you down.

But when you ask them,
Ask them, "How?"
It falls on deaf ears.
They say if you don't,
Then you're just going to end up
An Angry BLACK WOMAN.

But when you ask

Ask them
"How"
How to let go of the hurt
The hurt you never wanted
In the first place

They say
Nothing
And leave you to your own devices
They say
They don't know how
But if you need help, just reach out

They say
I am stronger than this
Because I am a Woman
But that's where they are wrong
I am stronger than this
Because I AM A BLACK WOMAN!

Love,
Whylde Chylde
March 4, 2019

The Crown of Love

The Crown I carry is heavy
With the weight of the Earth
From those that came before Me
And Myself.

Standing Tall.
It defies the Laws of Physics
Holding My Brothers Up
On the bones paralyzed by Life

Yet, I Decide
To Keep On Carrying.
Through Perseverance,
There is Strength.

Because I Am A BLACK Woman,
So I Am the Strength of the World!
From the Past,
To the Present.

I look to those before Me
To Guide Me Through Life

To Love and Uplift Myself
And My Community.

To Teach a Woman
Means to Teach a Nation.
Love a Woman,
So, She can Love Her Nation.

So, for I AM the Embodiment of Love.
And Only Through Love
Can you defeat the dark
It is in the darkness that you find hate.

So as Love,
I Must Stand Tall!
And wear My Crown
Because I cannot be beaten.

For I AM Love!

Love,
Whylde Chylde
February 19, 2019

The Day I Was Born

Where there is Death

There is Life

It is the light

And the dark

The day I found Death

There was no light

Only darkness

With the seed of Life taking ROOT

In Me

Because it was Death that I NEEDED

In order to be Born

To truly find Myself

I had to let go of Me

And since I couldn't

Death took me

Through understanding Death

Only then can you really understand Life

Because without Life

There is no Death

Where there is Life

There is also Death

The dark

To the light

It was when I figured out Life

Was I truly Born

But it was only through My Death

Could MY Life emerge

With the weight of Death

Lifted off MY Life

Only then could I Thrive

Because You can only Thrive in Life

Never in Death

Love,

Whylde Chylde

March 14, 2020

Mirror

When was the last time you looked at yourself

And got to know you

It's been a while for me

Even though you can usually find me behind some camera

I love the me that I imagine I'm going to be

I even love some of the pictures of me

But I don't like really looking at me

Especially in the mirror

I love looking at the me

Of who I will be

At least when I imagine

Me

I even love some of the moments

Of who I was

From the me

Captured in those moments

But I don't like really looking at me

The me of right now

And seeing who I currently am

With these brown almond-shaped eyes

And seeing more than this

Beautiful, sun-kissed melanin on me

But don't get me wrong

Have you seen this beautiful, brown sun-kissed skin on

me?

And it's not my heart

That can give freely

And worn on my sleeve

It's deeper than that

It's the me

Hiding behind my own eyes

Unsure if I want to see what lies within them

Scared of my own reflection

Tired of seeing the weight of my earth

In my eyes

Because then I find the stress of life

Wearing down my skin with these bags

I am more
More than my flaws
And I am more
More than my favorite parts of me

When I look at me
I should see
These captivating, honey, brown eyes
Holding both love and pain, equally

Seeing my side gap in my teeth
That I hate
All the while seeing them surrounded by all my dimples
Creating this amazing smile of mine

I need to see me, all of me
Mind, Body, and Soul
That is wrapped up in this deep
Rich, Brown skin of mines

I should be able to see myself

Even if no one else ever does

Because in Amerikkka

I will always be seen by my skin

I owe it to myself

To fully see myself

In all my glory

Filled with my own unconditional love

Love,

Whylde Chylde

May 20, 2020

Thrive

One day you're going to stop surviving

And you're going to start thriving

You'll never see it coming

You will just see when you get there

One day you will wake up

And you realize

That you're not the same person

Who had laid their head to rest

One day you're going to be happy

Smiling, laughing, and light-hearted

You're going to forget

All about that miserable girl

One day the person you are today

You won't be able to recognize tomorrow

That was someone who once was

But no longer is

One day you're going to love

The person you will become

You will allow her old self
To be a distant memory

One day you're going to be you
The new you
The one who is no longer surviving
You're going to be thriving

Love,
Whylde Chylde
March 2, 2019

Full Circle

I'm the type of person

Where I believe

Everything comes full circle

From

Who Is The Real Me

To The Story of Death

And The Day That I Was Born

Each of those

Are important to me

Because they help describe me

The many parts of me

That I couldn't access

Cause they wanted to hide

From me and the world

Buried deep

Dying of starvation

Wanting to be seen

Needing to be heard

In order to let go

Let go of the pain

And the past

But fully understanding
That everything comes full circle
Those written in a time of darkness
Thoughts of never being shared
But it's the light in the tunnel
That guides my path
Written by me to show me the way

The place of the Unknown
Only for me to create
Looking back to who I was
And how I got there
To looking forward
Finding my Birth
The keys to My Life in front of me

Everything comes full circle
The words of the past
Remind me
That everything happens for a reason
And it's all for me

I need it to get to where I'm going

It's the motivation
Of a Lifetime
Because it's My Lifeline
It's what gets me up in the morning
It is what pushed me for a better Life
A Life I deserve
Because I worked for it

Love,
Whylde Chylde
March 25, 2020

April Showers

April's showers bring May's flowers.

Do you know what's inside

Those April showers

They are the tears,

Of that little girl,

You know the one,

The one who's

Being touched

By her uncle and the brother.

It's the tears

From the little boy

Being touched by his babysitter.

It's the shame

From the girl

Who was frozen in place and couldn't say No

It's the boy

Who didn't know

That he could say No.

It's the teen
Who felt pressured
By their significant other.

And the one
Who was drunk.
With the one who wasn't.

April showers are made from tears
From those who have been violated,
Taken advantage of,

Molested,
Sexually Assaulted,
And raped.

Those tears water the seeds.
The seeds of their life,
So, they can bloom into flowers.

The beautiful May flowers

Of different types,

And different colors.

With longs petals,

And short ones,

Others filled and fully bloomed.

It is those tears

Inside April showers

That brings May's flowers.

I know this

Because #MeToo

I was 13, 22, and 23.

My April showers

Poured for years

Before they brought my May flowers.

And that is how I know

What is inside

Those April showers.

Love,

Whylde Chylde

April 3, 2020

I Stole This

I once heard
Someone say,
"I burned a few bridges
Back in my day.
Hell,
I burned my whole house down."

The person who heard this
Responded,
"Well,
You know what they say,
When your house burns down
You get a clear view of the sky."

So,
She responded,
"You mind if I steal that."
But little did they both know
I decided to steal all that,
The whole conversation.

I didn't steal that,

Because it sounded cool.
I stole that,
Because it touched
Touched me deeply.

From the beginning,
She said,
"I've burned a few bridges."
#MeToo.
I really felt that,
More than you will ever know.

She said,
"I've burned my whole house down."
And I looked around me
Stuck in an empty house.
One that is not my own
Cleaning out the mess.

And I thought back to
When I was drowning.
Trying to survive
Anyway, I could.

I ended up burning bridges
While drowning underwater.

And to the response,
"You know what happens
When your house burns down,"
And I just thought to myself
"No, what?" Immediately they said
"You get a clear view of the sky!"

Before it made sense to me,
It touched me.
I had thought back
Back to a time
When "The Sky is Falling"
Because it was lost

Instantly reminded,
That the wind is still there.
One breeze at a time
To a Destination unknown.
But that's the beauty of it,
There's nothing there.

There's nothing in the distance.

It's just pure vast space,

To be used,

To create,

And to imagine.

A whole new world, new beginnings

But then she said,

"You mind if I steal that."

At the same time, I thought to myself

I want that

I had already decided to steal that

And I wanted that too

So,

I stole that,

The whole conversation.

Because it touched me.

And I hope it touched you.

Always remember that

Yes, you can steal this too

Now,

Look Up To The Clear View of the Sky!

Love,
Whylde Chylde
March 24, 2020

Life Breath

As the breeze blows in the air,
Floating through the holes of your nose
The air finding its way down
Past your throat into your lungs.
You breathe in.

Lungs expanded,
Filled with the air
Carried through your veins
Reaching for your center.
You're alive.

Thoughts are processed
Creating the words,
The words of you
To be spoken by you.
It's the breath of life.

The air flows through You
Lifted up the canal of your neck
Passing through your lips
The words carried in the wind.

And you breathe out.

MAN-I-festation

The words of Your Man

Of Inner, Yourself pushed out

Into the world.

You thrive.

The air mixed

With Your words

Creating a powerful force

Because from the breath of life

Comes the words of life.

Love,

Whylde Chylde

May 18, 2020

Sex So Good

You ever had sex so good
with someone you weren't supposed to;
But, isn't that how it usually goes,
It's the people we are not supposed to fuck
That fucks us the best.

But, have you ever had sex sooo good
That, when you hear certain words like,
Compartmentalize or take this dick,
It brings you back to that night
And you can't help it.

Because it was soo good
That, you just get lost in it.
Every time.
You don't want to
Yet, you find yourself still doing it.

Have you had sex so good
That, when you think,
Think about their hands
Running up and down your body

With hands that are substantial.

They are substantial,

Both, in size

And in touch.

Because, when they finally landed on my neck.

Oh, when they finally landed...

It was like...

I don't even know

All I know is that,

That hand cradled my neck

Ohh, soo sweet.

With just the right amount of pressure

That it just held me there.

Gripping me firmly,

So, I could feel it.

But not enough to hurt.

Fingertips at my throat.

Palm under my chin.

But those hands,

They also held a softness to it.

Because I felt it.

I felt those big,

Soft man hands.

As they traced down my spine.

They touched me.

In a way, I haven't experienced it before.

So, those hands,

Oh, those hands

And those fingers.

They are something else.

They are a journey all on their own.

Because even now,

Talking about it,

It just does something to me.

Something I can't explain...

Other than, it just brings me back.

Like, have you ever had sex so good

That, you really only crave the sex.

And you only want to maintain

This type of relationship you have with them.

You don't want anything deeper than what it currently

is

But the sex is soo good

That you just want more of it.

And don't get me wrong, please don't,

Because I think their friendship is dope too.

But let's not forget about their sex,

Mmmmhmm, their sex.

I can't have one without the other.

But to be honest,

Do I even really want to,

Because their friendship is pretty cool,

But their sex is better.

Love,

Whylde Chylde

March 30, 2020

Shooting Star

We are born among the stars

A star to the signs and the planets

Traveling through galaxies across dimensions,

A soul.

My Soul, Your Soul

Together, we form the stars that shoot across the skies

Late at night,

Where Lovers meet

Families collide

It's the Union

Through the seasons, like Winter, Fall

The times and signs change

Planets transition

Lifetimes traveled

Always connected

Like your feet to the Ground

Keeping your body secure

Reminding you that you're just a star that landed

A star not quite yet ready for the next adventure

The next lifetime

Lifetimes of memories waiting to be unlocked
To further the Soul's journey
The Star on the move
Into the galaxies, the dimensions
Through the signs and planets
Flying across the skies

A Shooting Star

Love,
Whylde Chylde
October 8, 2020

Devil Eyes

Have you ever looked the devil in his eyes

Was it exactly how you imagined them

Dark, Cold, and Dangerous

Well, every time I saw the devil

His eyes were brown

Just like my own

Some held the blackness you were expecting

While others...

Well, you know how the saying goes

The one about the eyes

How the eyes are the gateway to the soul

Well, some souls had their devil buried deep

So deep that you never saw the devil coming

Only when it was too late

To escape the devil's grasp

Too late to save yourself

Before the devil got you and changed you

And then it was all said and done

Have you ever looked the devil in his eyes

The many eyes that he carries

Into the souls that he resides in

Because I have

I have seen too many devil eyes

And they aren't all the same

Love,

Whylde Chylde

December 16, 2020

Sea of Souls

Lone Soul

In the Sea of Souls

Lost among the others

Looking for a way out

Stuck to the physical

Of the typical

It is the light

And the end of the tunnel

That is hidden behind the funnel

Where all life crosses paths

In order to recognize themselves

Left behind from themSelves

Only to be found together

When one whole piece

Of the collective beings

Learn then share

It is the light

For all the lone souls

Lost in the Sea of Souls

Ascension past the physical

To the untypical

Place where

The Souls of the Light

Seeks the balance

To the lost souls in the Sea Souls

Love,

Whylde Chylde

August 16, 2020

Words

It's been so long

It feels as if it's been lost

Deep within the depths of my ocean

The place where all the sacred secrets are stored

Ready to be unlocked

And explored

No keys insight

For the locks on the door

But never locked away from myself

Cause its the words that flow

From My core

Through My Soul

My long-lost treasure that's never too far

But it's a million miles away

Farther than a star

Always within my reach

Grasped by my fingertips

Buried deep within

It's the words of My Soul
Getting lost from the traveling
That came from My Hearts desires

Love,
Whylde Chylde
January 1, 2021

Made in the USA
Middletown, DE
16 February 2022

61160426R00060